101
DEVOTIONS
FOR GUYS

From the Lives of
Great Christians

Copyright © Rebecca Davis 2017
ISBN: 978-1-78191-982-8

Published by Christian Focus Publications Ltd,
Geanies House, Fearn, Tain, Ross-shire,
IV20 1TW, Scotland, U.K.
Tel: 01862 871011
Fax: 01862 871699
www.christianfocus.com
email: info@christianfocus.com

Cover design by Tom Barnard

Printed and bound in China

101 DEVOTIONS FOR GUYS

From the Lives of Great Christians

REBECCA DAVIS

CF4•K

DAY 1

"Dick, will you come up and tell everyone about how Jesus Christ saved you?"

Fourteen-year-old Dick McLellan blushed deep red. He was so shy, he would almost rather die than speak in front of a crowd of strangers on a street like this! But he had first heard the gospel from these two ladies who smiled at him encouragingly now. Now, somehow, he told those strangers what God had done in his life.

Dick had no idea at that time, but God was going to call him to be a missionary from his home in Australia all the way to Ethiopia. There he would speak to huge crowds and dangerous criminals, he would face death many times over, and he would take the gospel where it had never been heard.

For all who will answer God's call, the Christian life is a great adventure. Every one of us can be a bold warrior in the army of God.

"One generation shall commend your works to another, and shall declare your mighty acts." Psalm 145:4

Thank You, Lord, that I can learn to be brave for You. Help me to trust You step by step as I declare your mighty works to others.

DAY 2

Joseph Flacks was a wealthy owner of a clothing factory. But a little girl who sewed buttons on clothes invited him to go hear an evangelist speak. He heard the gospel and trusted in Jesus Christ.

But then he lost everything! He lost his riches, he lost his social standing, and even his wife left him.

"When I went to Bible school," Joseph Flacks told a crowd, "The only work I could find to pay my bills was the lowest, most disgusting job in society. I cleaned streets at 2:00 every morning."

In those days, in the early 1900s, there were no cars on the streets. Everyone traveled by horse and carriage. In the cities there were many, many horses and carriages. Horse manure on the streets became a terrible problem. Street cleaners were important workers, but what a disgusting job!

"Christ poured out His love on me," Mr. Flacks said. "I can at least give my dignity for Him."

....

"Jesus, knowing that the Father had given all things into his hands, and that he had come from God and was going back to God ... began to wash the disciples' feet ..." John 13:3-5

Thank You, Lord Jesus, for Your love. Help me to be willing to do the lowest jobs, the jobs that no one else wants, for Your glory.

....

DAY 3

Don Gibbons and Gordon Larson prepared for years to take the gospel to the tribal people of New Guinea. After they arrived, they slogged for five days through soggy marshes, scrambled over rocky cliffs, and trudged through freezing rain to get to a remote tribe.

But even after they arrived, they had to keep working: building a hut, clearing land for an airstrip in this mountainous area, chopping down trees, and using levers to push the large rocks out of the way. They used shovels and axes to hack at the hard dirt, dug up grass, moved loads of mud, and dumped piles of dirt to fill in the ruts to make a smooth path.

Does all that sound exhausting? Sometimes the work of God can be very hard. But they wanted to give these people the good news of the God who loved them and sent His Son to die for them. The hard work was worth it.

....

"And let us not be weary in well doing: for in due season we shall reap, if we faint not."Galatians 6:9 KJV

Lord, thank You that I can have a part in the gospel going out, so that people can know You. Help me to be willing to work hard in Your service. Help me not to be lazy.

....

DAY 4

"Who do you worship?" missionary George Boardman asked the Karen people of Burma in 1828.

When the Karen people said, "No one," George thought they were atheists.

But he was wrong. The Karen tribe believed in one greatest God, Yuwah, but their ancient stories told them that He had gone far, far away, too far for them to worship.

It took George Boardman and other missionaries quite some time to find that out. When they did, they also found out there were other important beliefs in the Karen culture—for example, one tradition said that a "pale brother" would come from across the water with good news for them!

Do you know any people with a confused religion? Maybe they think that God is far, far away from them so they can't really draw near to Him. But the good news is that God is near—He has come close in the person of the Good Shepherd, Jesus Christ.

....

"The LORD is near to all who call on him, to all who call on him in truth." Psalm 145:18

Lord God, thank You that You are near to those who call out to You. Help me to carry this good news to others.

....

DAY 5

Have bad thoughts ever come into your mind that you wished you could be rid of?

This happened to Marco Franco in Colombia. Enemies who used to be his friends had nearly killed him because he was a Christian. His body recovered, but his heart struggled because he wanted to hate his attackers. Thoughts kept coming into his mind about getting revenge.

Over and over Marco asked God to forgive him and help him to love his enemies, but the thoughts just kept coming back. He sank into deep depression and despair. "How can I possibly even be a Christian?" he thought.

"Marco," said Pastor Vicente, "this is an attack from Satan. It is no sin to be tempted. It is a sin to welcome the temptation."

Marco was able to stand against the temptation and recover in his spirits. God helped him to love his enemies, and when he did, he was able to lead many to Christ.

....

"In all circumstances take up the shield
of faith, with which you can extinguish
all the flaming darts of the evil one."
Ephesians 6:16

Heavenly Father, help me to remember that
it is no sin to be tempted, only to welcome
the temptation. Thank You that I can resist
temptations through the shield of faith in
Jesus Christ.

....

DAY 6

"I can't believe how these Christians pray!" Saeed muttered. "They pray as if they're talking to a real person!"

Saeed was a faithful Iranian Muslim, but now he stood in the Christian pastor's house. He was supposed to tutor Pastor Yohannan in the Persian language, but he had to wait for the pastor and his friend to finish praying.

"They're not just reciting prayers they memorized," Saeed thought. "They even pray for their enemies! No good Muslim would do that! This is different from any religion I've ever seen!"

Do you ever pray for your enemies? That's hard, for sure. But Jesus said:

> "I say to you, Love your enemies and pray for those who persecute you."
> Matthew 5:44

The enemies of the Christians were the Muslims, Saeed's own people. But listening to the Christians pray for their enemies was the first step for Saeed in learning what Christianity really was. He learned that love is stronger than hate, and the love of Christ is the strongest of all.

....

O God, I pray that You'll teach me that love is stronger than hate. Give me a heart to love my enemies and bless and pray for the ones who persecute me.

....

DAY 7

"How can this be?" Saeed the Muslim muttered. "That Christian man is always kind and patient and truthful. He talks about the love of God, and he shows it. His whole life reflects all that he teaches! He never speaks badly of my people or my religion, though we speak badly of his people and his religion all the time! Why is this unbeliever so good, and we, the faithful Muslims, are not?"

Saeed's agony came because he saw the fruit of real Christianity in the life of Pastor Yohannan. Real Christianity isn't just about believing certain facts. It's about having a transformed life. That's what today's Bible verse means.

Because Saeed saw the gentle and loving life of Pastor Yohannan, and because he read the Bible and saw that Jesus was better than Mohammed, he gave the Lord Jesus his whole heart and soul. His life was completely transformed too.

....

"Abide in me, and I in you. As the branch cannot bear fruit by itself, unless it abides in the vine, neither can you, unless you abide in me." John 15:4

Dear God, thank You that I can go beyond just believing facts. Thank You that I can abide in You and bear fruit. Work in me, by the power of Your Holy Spirit to help me to be like Jesus.

....

DAY 8

When George Mueller was grown, he loved and served God. But when he was young, he didn't care about God at all.

Being a pastor was an easy way to make a good living, though, so that's what George's father wanted him to do. George went off to school where other boys were also preparing for Christian work. But none of them cared about God, or the sacrifice of Jesus on the cross, or the Bible.

God has something to say about people like this.

In Matthew 15:8 Jesus says, "This people honors me with their lips, but their heart is far from me; in vain do they worship me ..."

God sees the heart, and He knows when the praises on a person's lips aren't real.

What about the praises on your lips? Are you anything like the boys in George's school, studying about God but not caring anything about Him?

Now is the time to talk to Him about that, and ask Him to change your heart.

....

Father, thank You for the warnings You give in Your Word. Help me to live for You for real, truly wanting to seek after You.

....

DAY 9

George Mueller began to feel guilty about all the bad things he was doing while he was studying to become a pastor. "I'll stop stealing, cheating, lying, and getting drunk," he promised himself. "I'll become a better person."

For a few days he really did seem to be a better person. Then it felt like it was just too hard to be good, and he fell into his old sinful habits. He tried again to get back up. Then he slid back down again. Tried again. Slid down again.

Has your life ever felt like that? Have you ever tried to stop a certain sin problem, but then you go back to it? That's the life Paul talked about.

"I do not do the good I want, but the evil I do not want is what I keep on doing."
Romans 7:19

But the Bible also says that the righteousness of the law can be fulfilled in those "who walk not according to the flesh but according to the Spirit." Romans 8:4

George Mueller eventually found this out.
He trusted in Christ and had victory over his
sin. You can too.

....

Heavenly Father, thank You that through
the power of the Holy Spirit, I can have
victory over my sin. Help me to keep
trusting You for that victory.

....

DAY 10

In Ethiopia, Shaga the witchdoctor expected his son Nana to one day take his place. But when Nana was only twelve, he became a Christian. Shaga was furious and insisted that Nana turn from Christ and turn back to the way of the evil spirits.

How can a son honor a father who is wicked?

Nana had to follow the Lord. He couldn't obey his father, but even though he refused to obey, he never spoke disrespectfully to his father. This took tremendous courage, but the Lord helped him.

Sometimes the authorities in your life do wrong. When you have to choose to obey God rather than man, you can still show honor by speaking respectfully. Sometimes you may want to yell or be sarcastic, but you can ask the Lord to help you bite your tongue. It will take tremendous courage. Keep calling on Him to help you respect your authority even when you can't obey.

....

"We ought to obey God rather than men."
Acts 5:29 KJV

Thank You, Lord, that Your Holy Spirit
strengthens Your people to do right.
Help me to be respectful even when I
can't obey.

....

DAY 11

When Nana believed in Jesus, he refused to become a witchdoctor like his father Shaga. Even through his father's beatings and other cruel treatment, he stood fast and refused to deny Jesus.

Nana was only twelve years old.

Eventually Nana grew up to become a great evangelist in Ethiopia, telling many people about Jesus, His death on the cross for their sins, His glorious triumph over death, and His love for them. The gospel spread like a wildfire around the country, and this evangelist who had endured much was a part of it. One day even his father trusted Jesus.

If you know Jesus personally, He'll give you the strength to endure much, even through great trials and persecution. Don't give up! Keep trusting Him! He has called you to a great and important work, to give His gospel to many.

....

"Be watchful, stand firm in the faith, act like men, be strong."   1 Corinthians 16:13

Heavenly Father, I trust You to give me the strength to stand strong in You even through persecution, and do Your will, like Christians through history.

....

DAY 12

When he was saved, Marco Franco's life changed miraculously. God told him, "You are my child, and I love you." He changed from living for himself to living for God and others.

But then, because of his new faith in Jesus, Marco was beaten almost to death. And temptation came! How could his former friends do that? How could a loving God let this happen?

Would you be angry against people who had beaten you like this?

The tempter came, speaking evil words to Marco. "You're no Christian. No Christian would want to hurt his enemies like you do." A storm raged in Marco's heart.

But Marco knew he was forgiven and loved. Finally he was able to resist the devil by speaking truth, he forgave his enemies, and God delivered him from his dark thoughts.

Sometimes the enemy might whisper evil words to you too. But you can stand against the devil and trust in God and His truth.

....

"Resist the devil, and he will flee from you."
James 4:7b

Heavenly Father, thank You that You are stronger than the power of evil. Help me to resist the devil and his temptations in my life.

....

DAY 13

Many Christians were imprisoned for their faith in Ethiopia. But for some reason, God chose for the evangelist Nana to be invisible to the policemen. The guards didn't even see him when he took food and Scriptures to the prisoners.

Nana and the imprisoned Christians were both puzzled. But that's the way God did it.

Does that seem unfair? We can't always understand the ways of God, but we can know that God has different jobs for different Christ-followers. He may call some to suffer for Him and call others to work for Him. What's more, God's call might change. Later in his life, Nana served God from inside a prison. Other Christians were freed, and some were never imprisoned at all.

If you're struggling, thinking God is unfair to you, remember God loves you and cares about you. He has a good plan. Your story isn't over, and the one writing it is the best Author in the world.

....

"In [your salvation] you rejoice, though
now for a little while, if necessary, you have
been grieved by various trials." 1 Peter 1:6

Thank You, God, that You always have a
good plan. Help me to trust You with Your
good plan, even when life seems unfair.

....

DAY 14

When six thousand people gather outside to hear the gospel and there are no microphones, what's an evangelist supposed to do?

This is the problem the evangelists faced in Papua, Indonesia. So many people wanted to hear the gospel at once!

The Lord gave a creative solution. One Papuan evangelist stood in the middle of the crowd and began preaching, one line at a time. All through the crowd, other "echo preachers" stood. The ones close enough to hear him echoed his words. Then the ones farther out spoke, and on and on. That way, everyone in the crowd got to hear all of the gospel.

Would you have thought of solving this problem in that way? Sometimes challenges present themselves in our work for God, but God sees problems as opportunities for us to ask Him for a solution. If we seek Him in our service, He'll give us wisdom to find answers to our challenges.

....

"Commit thy way unto the LORD; trust also in him; and he shall bring it to pass."
Psalm 37:5 KJV

Thank you, Father, for all the good ideas You give people! Help me to be open to creative solutions You have for my problems.

....

DAY 15

Since the Karen people thought the true God, Yuwah, had gone far away from them, they thought they had to deal with the evil spirits themselves. And there were plenty of them. Spirits of the trees, weather and gardening, hunting, war, life, and death. They spent almost all their time trying to appease these nats, with prayers and offerings.

Appeasement looks sort of like worship, but it isn't really. Worship is full of love and thanksgiving, but there's no love in appeasement, only fear.

For the Karen people, though, the nats took the place of God—they thought and worried about them all the time. The nats became like little gods to them.

Maybe you know someone who is practicing appeasement. Maybe they're afraid of something in the spirit world, or maybe they're afraid of a person. But somehow, that thing or that person has taken the place of God. That somebody in your life needs help.

. . . .

"You shall have no other gods before me."
Exodus 20:3

Dear Lord, please show me how to help my friend who is living in fear and practicing appeasement. Help my friend to know the truth of what it's like to worship a God of love.

. . . .

DAY 16

Because the Franco family had become Christians, their enemies tried to burn their house down, with them in it. But miraculously they escaped.

Everyone was shocked to hear that they were now living in another town. But even more, they were shocked to hear that the Francos loved their enemies and wanted to do good to those who had tried to kill them. Their new faith in Jesus Christ was a sure faith, a faith for which they would willingly suffer.

"How can this be? How can they be willing to die for this faith and love the ones who tried to kill them?"

Secret believers began to announce their faith. "I'm a Christian. I'll host the church meetings in my home." Around the house that stood blackened and destroyed, new families declared their faith in Jesus Christ.

True Christianity is a sure faith in a sure Savior who works through radical love and peace.

....

"Truly, truly, I say to you, whoever hears my word and believes him who sent me has eternal life. He does not come into judgment, but has passed from death to life." John 5:24

Thank You, God, for Your sure faithfulness! Help me to have this radical love and peace.

....

DAY 17

Rajab had been studying the Koran with the greatest teachers in his area, but the more he learned it, the more full of confusion it seemed. For a time he wandered in great darkness, but then he decided to go listen to what a missionary said about Christianity. The last night, the missionary said, "Sin is like a terrible disease. All of mankind has this disease. There is only one medicine for it, and that's the gospel of Jesus Christ. You can accept this medicine, or you can reject it."

After more prayers and searching, Rajab decided to accept the medicine, and he was so glad he did. He was lifted from agony to joy. He was born again.

If you're struggling with a secret sin, the answer for you is the same. Even if you're already a Christian, the medicine that you need is still Jesus Christ. He can deliver you from your terrible disease.

....

"And when Jesus heard it, he said to them, 'Those who are well have no need of a physician, but those who are sick. I came not to call the righteous, but sinners.'"
Mark 2:17

Lord Jesus, thank You that You offer the perfect medicine for sin. Help me to keep trusting You to deliver me from my sin and make my life a new one, full of joy.

....

DAY 18

George Mueller was studying to become a pastor, but it was in a home meeting that he first heard the truth of the gospel.

"For God so loved the world, that he gave his only begotten Son, that whosoever believeth in him should not perish, but have everlasting life." John 3:16 KJV

All his life, George had known that Jesus had died on the cross. But now, for the first time, he understood why it was important. He knew that he must be forgiven of his sins through Jesus' death on the cross. For the first time, George understood that Jesus loved him and died for him. He trusted in Him, personally.

Maybe you've heard about Jesus all your life too. But just believing facts about Jesus and the Bible doesn't save you or make you a Christian. You must come to Him with your own personal sin and trust in Him to be your own personal Savior.

George became a true Christian. His life was radically changed.

....

Heavenly Father, thank You for sending Your only begotten Son, Jesus, to take my sin for me and rise again for me. Help me to trust Him for my own personal salvation, for all eternity, and day by day.

....

DAY 19

When the peddler spoke, everyone was amazed. "Away in another village, there is a man who can make you into a new person!" Two of the listeners decided they wanted to find this man, so they walked for three days to find him. They found a missionary to Ethiopia, Dick McLellan.

"I'm not the one who can make you new," Dick said, "but I know the one who can." For days he told them about Jesus.

Jesus loves to make people new. He's in the business of changing hearts and transforming lives.

Finally the two men trusted in Jesus. They became new on the inside, loving Christ and loving others, and it began to show on the outside as their faces and their lives were transformed.

Do you know that you're a new person in Christ? If not, keep looking to Him in faith, and trusting Him to accomplish this work in you.

....

"If any man is in Christ, he is a new creation. Old things are passed away, behold, all things are become new."
2 Corinthians 5:17 KJV

Thank You, Lord, that You make all things new! Show me how to trust You to do that in my life, through the power of Your Holy Spirit.

....

DAY 20

In Africa in the 1920s, Africans had to ride on the train third class. That meant they rode on an open flat car at the back. When the train needed to stop for fuel, all the third-class passengers had to jump down and chop wood.

This is discrimination, and it's against the law almost everywhere nowadays. But that's the way it was in those days.

In 1923, when Margaret Laird rode the train into Africa to be a missionary, she looked out of her second-class car to see the director of her mission board, Mr. Haas, riding third class. He was preaching to the Africans about Jesus, and teaching them a song about His great salvation. When it came time to chop wood, he jumped down in the heat and chopped wood with them. They sang together as they worked, even in the terrible heat. He knew he wasn't any better than the people he gave the gospel to.

....

"There is neither Jew nor Greek, there is neither slave nor free, there is no male and female, for you are all one in Christ Jesus."
Galatians 3:28

Thank You, Lord, that the ground is level at the foot of the cross. Help me to remember that I'm no better or worse than anyone else.

....

DAY 21

José desperately wanted power. He read in the New Testament about the power of the apostles and the power of Christ. "I want this power!"

"I'll become one of those *evangélicos*. I won't smoke or drink, and I'll spend all my time reading the Bible." But the darkness and fear didn't leave. Instead of power, he sank into depression. Where was the joy the Bible promised?

The way of Christ's power isn't found by rules.

"I know. I'll speak those magic words that I used before to call up that evil spirit—" but his whole body felt sick at the thought. He knew that way led to death.

The way of Christ's power isn't found in special words.

José cried out, "God! Release me from this terror!" He went to the Christian meeting and sang with them, "Oh, I want to walk with Christ." Then the Lord freed him and filled him. José found power to become a new man.

....

"But you will receive power when the Holy Spirit has come upon you, and you will be my witnesses in Jerusalem and in all Judea and Samaria, and to the end of the earth."
Acts 1:8

Lord God, others may promise me power, but You have said that the true way of power is found by faith in Christ alone. Help me to walk in that way.

....

DAY 22

What would it be like to live in a group of people who honor lying and deceit?

When Don Richardson went to the Sawi tribe of Indonesia, he found out. They told him about the men who were the best deceivers. The best kind of deceit, to them, was getting the enemy to think he was his friend, and then killing him. They laughed and laughed about those stories. But they lived in fear that their enemies would do the same to them.

This sounds shocking, but there are people like this in your own country. They would love to make you think they care about you, when really they're your enemy. This is the way Satan works.

When the Sawi tribe believed the gospel, they became honest and trustworthy and no longer lived in fear. Jesus wants this of us—it doesn't matter if our enemies are lying and deceiving. We want to be honest and trustworthy like Jesus.

....

"Lying lips are an abomination to the LORD,
but those who act faithfully are his delight."
Proverbs 12:22

Lord, help me to live faithfully and speak
truthfully. Help me to live a life of honesty
instead of deceit.

....

DAY 23

Nobody could ever trust anything the Sawis said. But Don Richardson found out there was one honest custom, called the Peace Child. When people from the two Sawi villages exchanged babies, they would have peace as long as the peace child was alive.

Don Richardson saw a great opportunity. He told the Sawi men that the Greatest Spirit had sent His own Son to be the Peace Child of the world. Because He rose from the dead, He would always be alive to bring peace to the heart of anyone who would trust Him.

If you've heard the story of Jesus all your life, you may not think it's amazing. But imagine these men hearing for the first time that there is an eternal Peace Child, and that they can have peace with the Greatest Spirit. Many Sawis trusted in the Peace Child of God, and today, the Sawi tribe is a Christian tribe.

....

"And a harvest of righteousness is sown in peace by those who make peace."
James 3:18

Thank you, Father, for sending Jesus to die for our sins. Thank you that He is the eternal Peace Child of God and we can always find peace with You through Him.

....

DAY 24

"Teacher Judson paid my debt and set me free." Those were the words of Thabew, a man of the Karen tribe, to missionary George Boardman.

The "Teacher Judson" that Thabew referred to was Adoniram Judson, who had come as a missionary to Burma years before. When Adoniram gave Thabew the gospel and Thabew believed, Adoniram Judson did what he could to release Thabew from captivity.

Thabew had a great debt, having murdered over thirty people. Money could never really fully pay it. But Adoniram Judson cared, and wanted to teach him and help him to grow as a Christian.

"He paid my debt and set me free." Ultimately, this is no truer of anyone than it is of Jesus Christ. Through His death on the cross, Jesus Christ paid Thabew's debt in full and set him free from slavery to those rages that had caused him to hurt so many.

....

"So if the Son sets you free, you will be free indeed." John 8:36

Lord Jesus, thank You that you have paid the debt of everyone who trusts in You. You have set us free from slavery to sin. I worship You for what You have done!

....

DAY 25

Thabew, a member of the Karen tribe, was a new Christian. But he wasn't baptized immediately, because he still had a violent temper. Before he was saved, Thabew's rages had caused him to murder many people. Now that he was a Christian, even though he didn't kill anyone, he still sometimes burst out into rages.

Thabew knew he couldn't be used of God the way he wanted to be until this problem was conquered. George Boardman prayed with Thabew for him to be delivered from his violent temper.

As time passed and Thabew trusted in Christ more, God did a transforming work. The rages that struck out against others changed. Instead, they became a passion against the kingdom of darkness, to see others delivered from slavery to sin. Thabew was eventually baptized and became a fervent evangelist.

....

"Let all bitterness and wrath and anger and clamor and slander be put away from you, along with all malice." Ephesians 4:31

Lord, I long to see rages against others changed to anger against evil. May I see souls delivered into the kingdom of Your dear Son. Do this in me and in the people around me, I pray.

....

DAY 26

William Miller read from the gospel of John to the Muslim men in the marketplace. "'As Moses lifted up the serpent in the wilderness,' " he read, "'even so must the Son of man be lifted up.' That means that Jesus had to die on the cross," he added.

"No, that's ridiculous," interrupted the men, waving their hands. "That's the foolish notion of the Christians. Your book is corrupted. Everybody knows Jesus didn't really die on the cross. Why would a prophet die on a cross?" They walked away. "But that's the way God made for our sins to be cleansed and for us to have eternal life," William thought. But they were gone.

Many people think that the Word of the cross is foolishness, but it isn't. Anyone who has believed in that Living Word, Jesus Christ, has experienced the power of God. Those who haven't will not know eternal life.

"For the word of the cross is folly to those who are perishing, but to us who are being saved it is the power of God."
I Corinthians 1:18

Lord Jesus, help me to see that the Word of Your cross is the way to eternal life in You. Help me to be faithful in giving that Word to others, even when it seems that they don't want to listen.

DAY 27

William Miller had to stay in a desert city in Persia (Iran) for two years. He gave out the Word of God there, but saw no one come to Christ. The whole place seemed like a spiritual desert too.

Twenty years later William returned to that city and found that a Persian chief had come to Christ and was telling others about Jesus. "I learned about Him from the Bible that I got from you," said the chief. "Twenty years ago."

When you tell others about Jesus, you may feel discouraged that no one is listening. But remember that what you're doing is sowing seeds. You may be the very first person to tell them about Jesus, or the tenth. But as long as your life matches with your words, your words will bear fruit, maybe even where you least expect it! Someday one of those people may say, "You were one of the reasons I came to Jesus. Thank you."

....

"Be patient, therefore, brothers, until the coming of the Lord. See how the farmer waits for the precious fruit of the earth, being patient about it, until it receives the early and the late rains." James 5:7

Thank You, Lord, that even when it feels like no one is listening to the gospel, You still have Your people who You're calling to Yourself. Please help me to remember that.

....

DAY 28

George Mueller wanted to bring glory to God by helping the many orphans who begged on the city streets, but he wanted to follow the Lord's leading, and he didn't want to ask anyone for money. So he prayed and prayed, asking the Lord to show him what to do.

One day George was reading in the Book of Psalms. In it, God said,

"Open your mouth wide, and I will fill it."
Psalm 81:10

George saw that God wanted to provide everything he would need for the orphans.

And God did provide. He provided the building, the supplies, and even the people, to take care of many orphans. George never asked anyone for money—every day he prayed for the things they would need the next day. For seven years God provided everything they needed, day by day.

Are you willing to trust the Lord like this? The Lord wants to show Himself strong for those who are willing to trust Him for His glory.

....

Thank You, Lord, that You want to do great things for those who trust You day by day. Show me how to trust You for my needs step by step in my life.

....

DAY 29

More and more people began to find out that George Mueller cared for orphans without ever asking for money. More and more people began to send him money to help with this important work.

What would you do if many people were sending you money for the Lord's work? Would you treat it carefully? Would you use it only to buy the things that are needed for the work of the Lord? Would you be faithful, or would you try to secretly take some of it for yourself?

George kept a record of every single penny he received, and how it was spent for the work of God. He wanted his life to show the glory of God, so this was very important to him.

By the end of his life, millions of dollars' worth of goods and money had gone through his hands. And he was faithful in every little bit.

....

"One who is faithful in a very little is also faithful in much, and one who is dishonest in a very little is also dishonest in much."
Luke 16:10

Lord, thank You for examples of faithfulness like George Mueller. Help me to be faithful in the work You've called me to do, as he was.

....

DAY 30

Dick McLellan and his friend Setta were taking the gospel to a far village of Ethiopia. It was a hard trek of many hours in terrible heat, climbing up a steep mountain, scrambling over rocks, and down the other side. Then they came to the violently rushing river. How would they ever cross?

Sometimes the way that God calls us can be long and hard and discouraging.

"Satan is trying to stop us!" Setta cried. "There must be a great victory ahead!"

They made it across the river. At the village, they saw God do a mighty work of salvation—even in the murderous witchdoctor! Then Dick was no longer sorry he had made that long, hard trek. He was no longer discouraged.

You can have great hope too, as you follow Jesus, even though your journey may sometimes seem long and hard. Don't give up. Remember if you feel discouraged in His way, He has victory ahead!

....

"I will instruct you and teach you in the way
you should go; I will counsel you with my
eye upon you." Psalm 32:8

Thank you, Father, that You lead Your
people in the way You want us to go. Help
me to trust You when the way seems hard.

....

DAY 31

Setta led Dick McLellan to the far village where a Christian named Wagaso had already brought many to Christ. Then when Dick preached, many people came to Christ, even the witchdoctor. Setta could help the witchdoctor better learn the way of truth, because he was the son of a witchdoctor. Wagaso forgave the witchdoctor for the evil he had committed and discipled him.

God used Dick, Setta, and Wagaso in different ways to proclaim and teach the gospel of Jesus Christ.

In 1 Corinthians 3:6, Paul said, "I planted, Apollos [another Christian] watered, but God gave the growth."

Every Christian has an important job in furthering the kingdom of God. You may not always see the results of your work for God, but if you're faithful in "planting" or "watering" or whatever part of Kingdom growth He has called you to, He will bring the fruit, in the hearts and lives of people.

....

Thank You, Father, that You call different Christians to different tasks. Show me the task You've called me to, and help me to be faithful in it.

....

DAY 32

Four-year-old Russell Stendal and his dad were reading a picture book. It showed how a people group in South America lived. The men spent all their money to get drunk, and the women and children had nothing to eat.

"Someone needs to go tell those people about Jesus!" Russell said. "We can do it."

His dad looked around at the comfortable living room and said, "But God has to call someone to be a missionary."

Russell kneeled down and prayed loudly, "God, please call my parents to be missionaries right now! I don't want to have to wait till I grow up to tell those Indians about Jesus!"

And God did. Four years later the Stendal family landed in South America as missionaries and began the adventure of a lifetime.

Comforts don't have to keep you from doing what God has called you to do. You can value the adventure of following God more than earthly comforts.

"Blessed be the God and Father of our Lord Jesus Christ, the Father of mercies and God of all comfort, who comforts us in all our affliction, so that we may be able to comfort those who are in any affliction, with the comfort with which we ourselves are comforted by God." 2 Corinthians 1:3-4

Father, help me to value the comfort You offer more than the comforts I can see.

DAY 33

Dick McLellan stuffed the old recording into his backpack. Twenty years earlier, this recording of the gospel story had been made in an unknown language of Ethiopia. The young man whose voice had been recorded had died shortly after, and no one could find the tribe he belonged to.

Then one day, when Dick was walking through the jungle, he took a wrong turn, leading him to a tribe hidden far away, secluded from everyone. He found that the tribe's language was the same one as this twenty-year-old recording. When they heard the gospel in their own language, many of them believed on the Lord Jesus Christ.

Sometimes the work of God can seem slow and long. But God's ways are not like our ways, and He is not in a hurry. He is accomplishing His good work in our lives and around the world, as long as we keep trusting in Him to do it.

....

"For my thoughts are not your thoughts, neither are your ways my ways, declares the LORD. For as the heavens are higher than the earth, so are my ways higher than your ways and my thoughts than your thoughts." Isaiah 55:8-9

Lord, show me how to trust You even when Your ways seem slow or confusing. Thank You that You always know what You're doing.

....

DAY 34

The tribal people burned the magic charms that connected them with the evil spirits. They said they wanted to be Christians. But the men still shook their long hair so the women would admire them. On their way to the church meeting, they broke into wild dancing and sang their old songs about chopping their enemies into little pieces.

Have you ever known anyone like that? Someone who said they were a Christian but talked about doing things that seemed very opposite to Christianity?

Maybe some of the men of the tribe wanted to change, but they were afraid to, thinking that they needed to be like all the other men, or like the leaders. Peer pressure happens all over the world.

Sometimes it's hard to follow Christ fully when people around you aren't doing it. But it's worth it. God hates hypocrisy, but He loves a heart that follows Him completely.

....

"Blessed are those who keep his
testimonies, who seek him with their whole
heart." Psalm 119:2

Dear God, please help me to follow You
with my whole heart, even when people
around me aren't.

....

DAY 35

After singing their songs about killing their enemies, the tribal men came to church.

"You say you want to follow Christ," the missionary John Dekker preached. "But your lives aren't matching up with what you claim. You need to beware. Jesus said,

"When the unclean spirit has gone out of a person, it passes through waterless places seeking rest, and finding none it says, 'I will return to my house from which I came.' And when it comes, it finds the house swept and put in order. Then it goes and brings seven other spirits more evil than itself, and they enter and dwell there. And the last state of that person is worse than the first."
Luke 11:24-26

Have you just swept out your house without inviting the Holy Spirit inside? You can go to church and sing without really worshiping. You can look like you're really paying attention, and speak politely. But

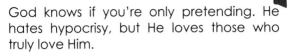

God knows if you're only pretending. He hates hypocrisy, but He loves those who truly love Him.

....

Lord God, help me to not just clean out the house, but also to invite the Holy Spirit to control my life. Thank You that You offer me that power.

....

DAY 36

One day before Sunday meeting, a handsome tribal man named Rigwi sat fingering his long black braided hair. The missionary told him his hair looked nice.

"Why do you speak good words about my hair?" Rigwi sneered. "Don't you know I grow my hair like this to shake it at the women and at the spirits? Why do you talk about it looking nice?"

Suddenly he stood up. "This hair is of the old way. I will get rid of it." He turned to the other Christians who had gathered. "You may want to keep your hair, but not me." Then to everyone's surprise he stomped away.

When Rigwi returned, his hair was gone. "I'm done with the old way," he said. "I want to follow the Jesus path."

Maybe something in your life is keeping you from following Jesus fully. Other people may not even realize that it's a hindrance to you, but you know, and God knows.

....

"(Jesus) saw a tax collector named Levi, sitting at the tax booth. And he said to him, 'Follow me.' And leaving everything, he rose and followed him." Luke 5:27-28

God, show me what is standing between me and You, like Rigwi's hair. Help me to get rid of anything that keeps me from following You with all my heart.

....

DAY 37

As the tribal people became more mature in their faith, they stopped the wild dancing and singing war songs before church meetings. Instead, they began to compose their own songs of worship to the mighty, loving Lord who had saved them.

"We love Jesus very much," they sang. "He died for us. His body was broken for us. His blood paid for our sins."

True worship is full of joy and thanksgiving. You worship God by thinking about how great He is and expressing your love for Him. He is "worthy"—that's where the word worship comes from. He is worthy of all of our praise and adoration. He is worthy of the offering of our very lives.

"We're thinking about the death of Christ," the people sang. "We're thinking that Christ will come. We will go to heaven to be with Him. We love Him very much."

....

"Worthy is the Lamb who was slain, to receive power and wealth and wisdom and might and honor and glory and blessing!" Revelation 5:12

Lord Jesus, thank You for dying for me. I worship You, because You are worthy.

....

DAY 38

Early in the morning, five men went together to the river. It was time for Thabew to be baptized, the very first Karen Christian.

When missionary George Boardman lowered Thabew into the water, he said, "I baptize you, my brother, in the Name of the Father and of the Son and of the Holy Spirit. You are buried with Him in the likeness of His death. You are raised with Him in the likeness of His resurrection."

The three Karen men watching were excited to hear George call Thabew "brother," because their old legends said that the lost white book would return with the pale younger brother from the West.

But they didn't understand the symbolism of baptism. Eventually George was able to explain that when Jesus Christ died, we died with Him. When He rose again, we rose with Him, to walk in a new life. It's a mysterious symbol, and a beautiful one.

....

"We were buried therefore with him by baptism into death, in order that, just as Christ was raised from the dead by the glory of the Father, we too might walk in newness of life." Romans 6:4

Lord Jesus, thank You for Your death and resurrection! Thank You that when You died, all those who believe in You died too, and when You rose again, we rose again in You.

....

DAY 39

Thabew was a new Christian when he became a missionary to his own people, the Karen tribe. He had only just been baptized, and he had almost no training. But he knew that the long-lost hope of the Karen tribe was near, that Yuwah had returned to them, and that Jesus Christ was the answer. He was glad to give his whole life for this important purpose.

God can use anyone who is willing to be used by Him. Though education can be a very good thing, what God wants most is a heart that is wholly devoted to Him.

"I understand you only a little," one of the Karen people said to George Boardman, the American missionary. "But I understand Thabew perfectly." Thabew was such an important messenger to His own people that he became known as the Karen Apostle.

Even now, if your life is devoted to God, God can use you. Trust Him to work in you through the power of His Spirit.

....

"Do not be conformed to this world, but be transformed by the renewal of your mind, that by testing you may discern what is the will of God, what is good and acceptable and perfect." Romans 12:2

Thank You, God, that You are pleased to use anyone whose life is dedicated to You! Help me to offer myself to You for You to use me in Your good work.

....

DAY 40

"You need to come help Chief Nacio," said Santiago. "He's dying."

"What will happen if I come but he doesn't get better?" missionary Chad Stendal asked.

"The people will kill you."

"Lord," Chad prayed, "should I go to Chief Nacio's village and risk my life to bring them the gospel? If You want me to go, I'll go, and if you want me to stay, I'll stay."

"Go!" said the Lord. His voice was like a powerful wind.

How can you hear God's voice in your own life? It begins with reading His Word and spending quiet time with Him. If you aren't hearing from Him, maybe you have too many distractions. Maybe you have sin in your life. Or maybe you're just not used to hearing him. Don't be discouraged if it takes time. Focus on Him and ask Him to give you clear leading. The Lord is always speaking, and He loves to speak to His children.

....

Jesus said, "My sheep hear my voice, and I know them, and they follow me." John 10:27

Thank You, Lord, that You speak, through Your Word and Your Spirit. Help me to learn how to listen for Your voice.

....

DAY 41

To get to the dying Chief Nacio, Chad Stendal climbed steep mountains, crossed rushing rivers, and edged along narrow paths that dropped off sharply.

When he ate the food that was given him, he didn't know whether it was poisoned. When he gave the chief medicine and prayed over him, he wasn't sure the chief would live.

Chad didn't know if the Lord would do something great, or if he would never return home. He just knew the Lord had called him to go, and he wanted to be faithful.

The apostle Paul often felt the same way. He was willing to go forward for the sake of God's Kingdom, but he said he was "often near death" (2 Corinthians 11:23).

If you don't feel this kind of boldness, don't lose heart. Ask God to build boldness in you day after day as you grow in Him, for the glory of His Name. He loves to use those who want to faithfully follow Him.

....

"The wicked flee when no one pursues,
but the righteous are bold as a lion."
Proverbs 28:1

Heavenly Father, thank You for examples
of boldness. Help me to be bold in going
forward for You.

....

DAY 42

It was a miracle! Chief Nacio, who had been almost dead, was not only alive, but walking toward Chad Stendal! He wanted to listen to the Bible stories in the Kogi language that Chad had brought.

"Those are real stories," the chief said, nodding. He called for all the Kogis from his area to come and listen.

And yet, the spiritual darkness was great, and the Kogis in other areas fought against the coming of the gospel. They were afraid, because of what Spanish explorers had done to their people hundreds of years before.

Even now, only a small percentage of the Kogi Indians in the Santa Marta Mountains of northern Colombia have believed in Jesus Christ. The others continue to live in darkness and fear. Will you pray that the Lord will send more courageous people to teach them the Truth and show them the Way and bring them the Light?

....

"Then [Jesus] said to his disciples, 'The harvest is plentiful, but the laborers are few; therefore pray earnestly to the Lord of the harvest to send out laborers into his harvest.'" Matthew 9:37-38

Lord of the harvest, please send out more workers to tell people about You. Help me to be willing to go if that's what You want me to do.

....

DAY 43

George Mueller never asked anyone except the Lord for money to care for the orphans. The Lord spoke to His people and gave him so much that George was able to build a huge house for many more orphans.

Someone in George's town wrote, "Whenever I doubted the Living God, I looked up in the evening. There on the hill I could see the many windows of the orphanage lit up. They gleamed out through the darkness like stars in the sky."

This man knew that every penny George received, he got only by asking God. The man added, "When I looked at that place, I was reminded that God is alive."

There are ways you can be reminded that God is alive too. He has done great things throughout history, and is doing them even now around the world, even where you live.

....

"Give, and it will be given to you. Good measure, pressed down, shaken together, running over, will be put into your lap. For with the measure you use it will be measured back to you." Luke 6:38

Heavenly Father, thank You for the ways that You show You're alive and active in the lives of Your people. Thank You that as we give to You and trust You, You provide the needs of Your people.

....

DAY 44

In the hospital with a high fever, Hossein tossed and turned in a fitful sleep. Then a voice called, "Hossein, I am Jesus Christ. Arise and eat." In his dream Hossein ate the food before him and felt stronger. In the morning he was well. He knew that Jesus had healed him.

Hossein found a Christian church and began to ask the pastor many questions. The pastor told him that in John chapter 6, Jesus said He was the Bread of Life, the source of strength. Hossein read and listened and studied and believed. He became a Christian.

For you, the source of your strength isn't the written Word of God, even though that's very important. The Bible points you to the source of your strength, the Living Word of God, Jesus Christ. He is the Living Bread from heaven. He promised that whoever eats from Him will have eternal life. That means you get spiritual strength and life by believing in Him.

"And Jesus said unto them, I am the bread of life: he that cometh to me shall never hunger; and he that believeth on me shall never thirst." John 6:35 KJV

Lord Jesus, I come to you again, asking you to fill me with Your living Bread. You are the source of all my spiritual strength. Thank You that I can arise and eat.

DAY 45

"You are a Muslim, and you will never be a Christian!" Hossein's uncle yelled. "You will renounce this Christianity!"

But Hossein had found true salvation in Jesus Christ. How could he deny Him?

His family begged and pleaded and threatened. Finally they rejected him.

When Hossein thought about how he no longer had a family to share love with, his heart was heavy. But he loved Jesus more.

Hossein traveled to the home of a Christian friend, and that family embraced him as a member of their own family. They told him that he was their spiritual brother.

Even if your own family members were to reject you for your faith in Christ, you could still find brothers and sisters in the faith. Because God is our Father, all of us who believe in Jesus Christ are brothers and sisters. If you've trusted in Jesus, you have a gigantic family!

....

Jesus said, "For whosoever shall do the will of God, the same is my brother, and my sister, and mother." Mark 3:35 KJV

Thank You, Lord, for the family You've given me. Thank you that my spiritual family extends far beyond my physical family.

....

DAY 46

Lying in the hospital were two men. One was a rich coffee trader; the other was Kebede, a poor man. The coffee trader knew Kebede's language, so he could translate for the Christians who gave the gospel. Kebede believed in Jesus and was saved.

But the coffee trader wasn't interested and went on his way, trusting in his riches. These men were like the men Jesus spoke about in Matthew.

Jesus said, "Everyone then who hears these words of mine and does them will be like a wise man who built his house on the rock." Then the terrible storms came, "but it did not fall, because it had been founded on the rock.

And everyone who hears these words of mine and does not do them will be like a foolish man who built his house on the sand." Then the terrible storms came, "and it fell, and great was the fall of it."
Matthew 7:24-27

In the end, riches can never save you. Only Jesus Christ can save.

....

Lord Jesus, help me to trust in You alone for all my salvation. Help me to trust You for my eternal salvation, and for moment by moment as you save me from the power of sin.

....

DAY 47

When God called the Laird family to be missionaries to cannibals in Africa, they drove the three hundred miles to the new outpost. But their new flock of goats – how would they get there?

Well, Kongi the goat boy walked those three hundred miles with the herd of goats.

Kongi knew and cared about those goats—he may well have known them all by name, just as Jesus does His sheep. Kongi knew how to care for them, when they needed feeding, milking, and watering.

Do you suppose the way may have been rough and hard and hot and tiring? The goats didn't understand why they had to leave their old home. But Kongi understood, and he led them safely all the way to their new home.

In the same way, Jesus leads us, even when we don't know where we're going. Along the way, it may seem confusing and difficult, but we can trust that He knows best and is leading us to a safe place.

....

"He will tend his flock like a shepherd; he will gather the lambs in his arms; he will carry them in his bosom, and gently lead those that are with young." Isaiah 40:11

Thank You, Lord, that You care for Your flock. Help me to trust You when the way seems unclear.

....

DAY 48

As the son of a witchdoctor, Siud was supposed to learn all the ways of the spirits. But Siud hated those spirits. They were spirits of fear and death and horror and hatred.

Siud stood on a mountain peak looking out over the river, out beyond the mountains. "There must be a spirit who loves," he thought. "There must be."

He listened to the sound of the raging river below him. "If my people find out what I'm thinking, they'll throw me in the river. But someday I'm going to find that Spirit who loves, and He's the one I'll follow."

Years later, when a kind missionary came, Siud thought he might be the Spirit who loves. But Phil Masters told him about the true God who sent His Son, Jesus Christ. Siud found out that the Spirit who loves was also more powerful than all the other spirits. He learned to love Him and talk to Him in prayer.

....

"So we have come to know and to believe the love that God has for us. God is love, and whoever abides in love abides in God, and God abides in him." 1 John 4:16

Thank You, Lord, that You are the Spirit who loves. Thank You that I can talk to You in prayer, and that You care about me.

....

DAY 49

"Hossein, you need to go to Bible school," his Christian friends told him. "The American missionary, William Miller, is teaching one in Mashhad."

"Bible school?" Hossein thought. It was like a dream. Getting to spend all day every day learning the Bible?

"But I can't do it," he said. "I don't have any money. How would I pay for a place to stay? How would I buy food?"

"Christians in the United States are sending money to William Miller," his friend said. "They want to help people in Iran learn the Bible. All of your needs would be supplied."

It sounded too good to be true, but it wasn't. Hossein went to Bible school in Mashhad. Day after day, he was able to "arise and eat" of the Word of God, learning and understanding who Jesus Christ really is and who he was as a Christian. He went on to become a great evangelist and pastor in his land.

....

"Each one must give as he has decided in his heart, not reluctantly or under compulsion, for God loves a cheerful giver." 2 Corinthians 9:7

God, thank you that the money we send to missionaries is used to help train people to take the gospel to others in their land. Help me to remember to continue to give as I can.

....

DAY 50

The people of the Karen village of Chikku had been given a book many years before. Now, because they honored books so much, they were worshiping it. There was even a man they called The Guardian of the Book. But nobody could read it. When the missionary George Boardman arrived they asked him to tell them what the book was.

It turned out to be a Book of Common Prayer. "It's a good book," said George "but you shouldn't worship it. Worship Jesus Christ alone." That very day the Guardian of the Book gave up his special robes and rod and turned to Jesus Christ.

Does it sound silly to you to worship a book? You might be surprised at how much this same kind of thing happens today. It can happen to a person without his even realizing it. People can exalt and honor a Christian leader or even the Bible so much that they're turning to something God made instead of to God Himself. Don't make that mistake. Worship Jesus Christ alone.

....

"And when I heard and saw [these things], I fell down to worship at the feet of the angel who showed them to me, but he said to me, 'You must not do that! I am a fellow servant with you and your brothers the prophets, and with those who keep the words of this book. Worship God.'"
Revelation 22:8-9

Lord God, when my heart turns to love and exalt something or someone more than You, show me. Help me to worship You alone.

....

DAY 51

If you were going to preach to someone who had never heard the gospel before, what Scriptures would you choose?

George Boardman preached to the Karen people of Chikku with simple gospel messages. "For God so loved the world that He gave His only begotten Son." "Believe on the Lord Jesus Christ, and you will be saved." "Come unto Me all you who labor, and I will give you rest."

The gospel isn't complicated. God made it very simple. God gave His only Son for you. He wants you to believe in Him to be saved. If you do come to Jesus Christ, you will find rest for your soul. Rest from trying to please God through works, and rest from trying to find happiness any other way. In Jesus Christ you can find a safe place. He will always love you, have compassion on you, and be glad to be with you.

....

Jesus said, "Come to me, all who labor and are heavy laden, and I will give you rest. Take my yoke upon you, and learn from me, for I am gentle and lowly in heart, and you will find rest for your souls. For my yoke is easy, and my burden is light." Matthew 11:28-30

Thank You, God, that Your gospel is simple and beautiful. Thank you that I can be filled with hope when I think about finding rest in Jesus Christ.

....

DAY 52

The country of Colombia was overrun with Communist revolutionaries—people who lived as outlaws, stealing and killing. Sometimes Russell Stendal flew his airplane over the jungles where they had their hideouts. "God, make a way for them to hear the gospel," he prayed.

Then Russell was kidnapped by these revolutionaries. "I've got to escape," he thought. "I need to be rescued."

What about your kidnappers? God said. Don't they need to be rescued? They've been taken prisoner in a different way. They don't know how to escape.

Russell realized God had brought him to people who needed to hear the gospel. His prayer was being answered.

Sometimes your circumstances may seem very difficult, but this might be the way God is going to do a great work and answer a prayer of your heart.

....

"And do not seek what you are to eat
and what you are to drink, nor be worried.
For all the nations of the world seek after
these things, and your Father knows that
you need them. Instead, seek his kingdom,
and these things will be added to you."
Luke 12:29-31

Lord Jesus, sometimes circumstances
look really hard. Help me to know that
You're accomplishing something good all
the time.

....

DAY 53

"I was wrong," Russell Stendal said. "I shouldn't have said I didn't have a gun. It was wrong to lie."

Communist revolutionaries had taken him prisoner in the jungles of Colombia. But now they looked at him in surprise. He was admitting that he had done something wrong? He was saying it was wrong to lie? They lied all the time, and they expected everyone else to lie too. This man was very different, that was for sure!

You don't have to be perfect to tell others about Jesus. But you do have to be a person who is willing to confess your sins and want to truly change, by the power of God.

The revolutionaries began to listen to Russell when he talked to them about God. One after another, they began to believe and trust in Him, more and more. Russell's life made a difference. The message of hope in Jesus Christ made an even greater one.

....

"If we confess our sins, he is faithful and just to forgive us our sins, and to cleanse us from all unrighteousness." 1 John 1:9

Dear God, thank you for Russell Stendal's example of honest confession and repentance. Help me to confess my wrongs to You and to the people my wrongs have affected. Help me to repent and change, through the resurrection power of Jesus Christ.

....

DAY 54

William Ready came from the streets of England to George Mueller's orphanage. When it was time for him to graduate and go on to be an apprentice with a Christian businessman, Mr. Mueller called him into the office. "William, you can hold tighter with your right hand than with your left, can't you?"

William was puzzled by this strange question. "Yes, sir."

Mr. Mueller put a Bible in William's right hand and a coin in his left hand. "Well, my boy," he said, "hold on tight to the teachings of that Book, and your left hand will always have something to hold."

What did he mean? Love the leading of the Lord through His Word, keep trusting Him through faith, and He will always provide for you.

William learned who Jesus really was, the Savior of the world, and his own personal

Savior. He became an evangelist in Australia to proclaim the Word of God there.

....

"How can a young man keep his way pure? By guarding it according to your word." Psalm 119:9

Thank You, Lord, that You lead us through Your holy Word. Help me to keep my way pure by following You.

....

DAY 55

Read this verse from 1 Corinthians:

"I protest, brothers, by my [boasting] in you, which I have in Christ Jesus our Lord, I die every day! What do I gain if, humanly speaking, I fought with beasts at Ephesus? If the dead are not raised, 'Let us eat and drink, for tomorrow we die.'"
1 Corinthians 15:31-32

When Paul talked about dying daily in I Corinthians, he wasn't referring to spiritual death—he was talking about physical death! He meant that he faced death every single day in his desire to tell people about the saving work of Jesus Christ.

This happens to missionaries all around the world too. Dick McLellan stood in front of Ethiopian warriors who were all pointing their guns at him. He knew he could die at any moment. But he said, "I have an important message for your chief." The warriors let him pass and take that message of the gospel.

Dick talked to the chief, he found that the chief had been waiting for years for the very message he was bringing.

Is it worth it? Is it worth it to offer your life, to "die every day"? Yes, it's worth it! There is no greater joy than to know that people have learned and embraced the Truth.

....

Lord, I pray that I'll be willing to give
my life for others to know You and the
great salvation they can have through
Jesus Christ.

....

DAY 56

Yun's mother lay in bed, halfway between wake and sleep. She wanted to die so much, she was even considering suicide. If her husband died of this terrible cancer, how could she go on living? Then she heard a clear voice speak from somewhere, with great kindness. "Jesus loves you," it said.

Yun's mother hadn't heard of Jesus in thirty years. In Communist China in 1974, everything about Jesus had been eliminated. All Bibles, mission work, even Christians. But thirty years earlier, Yun's mother had given her life to Jesus.

Now she prayed again, with her children, knowing that Jesus was their only hope. "Jesus! Heal Father!" they cried.

Within a week, Yun's father was completely cured of his cancer. Everyone in the family trusted in Him, and they secretly told the others in their village.

This was the beginning of a life of adventure for Yun, who would one day be better known as Brother Yun.

....

"May the God of hope fill you with all joy and peace in believing, so that by the power of the Holy Spirit you may abound in hope." Romans 15:13

Lord Jesus, You are my hope for my rescue, for eternity, and in this life. Please help me with the things I'm struggling with, and help me to continue to hope in You.

....

DAY 57

"Who is Jesus really, Mother?" Yun asked.

Yun's mother answered the best she could from the teaching she had received thirty years earlier. "The Son of God, who died on the cross for us. He took all our sins and sicknesses. His teachings were recorded in the Bible, but there are no more Bibles left."

In those days in China, if anyone was caught with a Bible, he and his family would be severely beaten, and the Bible would be burned.

For four months, Yun prayed for a Bible. He cried and cried and ate almost nothing.

Then one night, he dreamed that two men with a red bag whispered to him that they had bread. The next morning two men with a red bag stood at his door. Secretly, they gave him a Bible. It was Yun's first gift from God, and his second miracle. He took in the words of the Bible as a starving man eating bread.

....

"Your words were found, and I ate them,
and your words became to me a joy and
the delight of my heart, for I am called
by your name, O Lᴏʀᴅ, God of hosts."
Jeremiah 15:16

Thank You, Lord, for your Holy Word, the
Bible! Help me to love it and feed on it and
get to know You better through it.

....

DAY 58

When Russell Stendal was first taken prisoner, he struggled with wanting to get free. *Should I try to escape? Please rescue me, God!* Every night in his hammock when the flashlight shone in his face, he felt fear. But as time passed, he began to feel a heart of compassion for his kidnappers.

When Russell's family sent him a Bible, he began to mediate on a psalm every day. He even read the Bible out loud.

As the weeks turned to months, Russell prayed for his kidnappers to find true freedom in Jesus Christ, to be released from their captivity. Every night he prayed for hours.

Russell was focusing his heart on the Father. He had no way to know that God was going to use this kidnapping experience in an awesome way in the future, but he was patiently trusting God and waiting for Him to work in His time.

....

"And it is my prayer that your love may abound more and more, with knowledge and all discernment, so that you may approve what is excellent, and so be pure and blameless for the day of Christ, filled with the fruit of righteousness that comes through Jesus Christ, to the glory and praise of God." Philippians 1:9-11

Thank You, Lord, that You give opportunities even in hard times for us to focus on You. Help me to trust You in my hard times.

....

DAY 59

The revolutionary boasted to his prisoner, missionary Russell Stendal. "Communism will free all countries and solve all the world's problems. Then everyone in the world will have enough to eat, and we'll eliminate disease and poverty."

But Russell didn't believe him. "You're using murder and robbery and terrorism to try to bring world peace?" he asked. "I haven't done anything wrong, but you're holding me prisoner and you might kill me. How can you sow injustice and expect to reap justice? How can you sow bad things and expect to reap good things?"

Russell was referring to what the apostle Paul wrote in Galatians. This is true for you too. How can you expect to do wrong, without paying a price someday? How can you expect to get away with evil? You cannot. God sees and knows, and He will repay. Instead, live a life of repentance, coming to your senses every day to live in the light of God.

....

"The one who sows to his own flesh will from the flesh reap corruption, but the one who sows to the Spirit will from the Spirit reap eternal life." Galatians 6:8

God, sometimes Your law of sowing and reaping seems hard. But it's a good law, and so I thank You for it. Help me to come to my senses every day and turn to You, so that I can sow to the Spirit and reap eternal life.

....

DAY 60

Joy Ridderhof and Ann Sherwood trekked all over the world with their heavy, bulky recording equipment, recording as many tribal languages as they could. Sometimes the equipment didn't work, and then they couldn't make a recording.

But back at their office in California, some engineers and inventors were always trying to make better recording equipment. They made it smaller, lighter, and more efficient. Every time they invented something new, they were excited to send it to Joy and Ann.

There are so many jobs to do in the Kingdom of God. Some people are called to preach and teach. But many more are called to do other jobs, like inventing and fixing. Many people can help God's work behind the scenes, just by making equipment work the way it should. God delights in all the ways His children serve Him. No matter what your gifts or skills are, there are ways you can use them in the Kingdom of God.

....

"Bezalel and Oholiab and every craftsman in whom the LORD has put skill and intelligence to know how to do any work in the construction of the sanctuary shall work in accordance with all that the LORD has commanded." Exodus 36:1

Heavenly Father, thank you for the talents and skills You've given me. Show me how I can use them for Your Kingdom.

....

DAY 61

Dick McLellan set up his projector to display pictures on a sheet. He showed picture after picture of Jesus and explained who He was and what He did for us.

"If we trust Him," he said, "then we can stand before a holy God!"

But just as he was about to call for people to repent of their sins, someone saw a large "creature" on the sheet and started whacking at it. Others did too. Everyone started yelling.

By the time Dick realized it was just a little bug on the projector lens, everyone was in an uproar. "Should we quit?" he wondered.

"No, this is the work of the Enemy," whispered his friend. "Let's try again."

It was worth it. When Dick called for people to repent, many did. Even one of the most notorious murderers of that whole area trusted in Jesus.

Satan loves to use distractions to turn people's hearts away from Christ. Don't let him win.

....

"Give ear, O my people, to my teaching; incline your ears to the words of my mouth!" Psalm 78:1

Father in heaven, help me to keep You in my thoughts. Don't let Satan win the victory in my heart through distractions.

....

DAY 62

George Boardman lived and worked in a very difficult environment in Burma, without comforts of home. He died there when he was only thirty.

If George had stayed in America, he might have lived comfortably many more years. Why would anybody do something that appeared so foolish?

Jesus said, "For whoever would save his life will lose it, but whoever loses his life for my sake will save it. For what does it profit a man if he gains the whole world and loses or forfeits himself?" Luke 9:24-25

You can't keep your life—you'll die one day anyway. If you give your life for Christ, then He'll give you spiritual rewards, which can never be lost.

George Boardman was no fool. The last thing he saw was many new Karen Christians being baptized in the river. Some of his last words were, "Lord, now let Your servant depart in peace, for my eyes have seen Your salvation!"

....

Dear Father, thank You that You offer treasures that can never be lost. Help me to remember what's really important.

....

DAY 63

After George Boardman died, Francis Mason began the job of returning the White Book to the Karen people. Faithful young men helped him learn the Karen language, with all its strange new sounds and vocabulary. Then he made symbols to represent their sounds—an alphabet. He and his wife taught the men to read. They helped him translate the first book of the New Testament. He worked on all this for six years.

It sounds tedious! But finally, Mr. Mason produced the book of Matthew. The Karen tribe rejoiced to read the White Book of Yuwah in their own language.

But the work wasn't finished. Faithfully he continued another six years, translating the rest of the New Testament. More Karen people read it and trusted Christ.

But the work wasn't finished. Faithfully he continued another ten years, translating the Old Testament. Altogether, this work took twenty-six years. But the lives of the Karen tribe were forever changed. Being faithful was totally worth it.

....

"And what you have heard from me in the presence of many witnesses, entrust to faithful men who will be able to teach others also." 2 Timothy 2:2

Thank You, Lord, for faithful men who give their lives for You. Help me to be a faithful man too.

....

DAY 64

"Listen, Siud," missionary Orin Kidd said. "This is from the last book of the Bible, the book of Revelation." Orin read Revelation 7:9-10 in the Kimyal language,

"I looked, and behold, a great multitude that no one could number, from every nation, from all tribes and peoples and languages, standing before the throne and before the Lamb, clothed in white robes, with palm branches in their hands, and crying out with a loud voice, 'Salvation belongs to our God who sits on the throne, and to the Lamb!'" Revelation 7:9-10

Siud was stunned. "This means that people from all nations will praise Jesus Christ together? The Kimyals too?"

"Yes, the Kimyals too." It seemed almost too good to be true. People from all nations, tribes, and languages worshiping together around the throne of God!

If you've trusted in Christ as your Savior, you'll be worshiping with people from Indonesia, Ethiopia, Colombia and Iran and all over the world. What a day that will be!

....

Thank You, God, that You love to call people from all over the world, of all nations, tribes, and languages, to worship You. Thank You that they are all my brothers and sisters in Christ.

....

DAY 65

Missionary Russell Stendal was being held for ransom—as high a price as his kidnappers could get. One day one of the young men asked him, "What will you do if your family can't pay our price?"

"Well, I know they can't afford much," Russell replied. "So you could just take whatever they give you, or . . . you could kill me."

"But aren't you afraid to die?"

Russell shook his head. "I know it would be uncomfortable," he said. "But no, I'm not afraid."

The young man turned away soberly. How could anyone be unafraid to die? What kind of strength was this?

The strength that Russell had was the strength of knowing that the things he couldn't see were more real than the things he could see. He knew that trusting in Christ gave him a far better inheritance than trying to get things on this earth.

....

"For this light momentary affliction is preparing for us an eternal weight of glory beyond all comparison, as we look not to the things that are seen but to the things that are unseen. For the things that are seen are transient, but the things that are unseen are eternal." 2 Corinthians 4:17-18

Heavenly Father, help me to understand and know that the things I can see won't last, but the things that I can't see are eternal.

....

DAY 66

In 1979, the country of Iran underwent a massive revolution. The man who took over, the Ayatollah Khomeini, promised peace and plenty, but all he brought was violence and famine. The whole nation groaned under his harsh rule.

Now mission work was completely different. Now Christianity was illegal, and Christians had to meet in secret—it was extremely dangerous because they could be killed by the government. There were only a few hundred Christians in the country anyway. Surely Christianity would be completely wiped out.

Have you ever noticed that when terrible things happen, that's when people start really turning to God for help?

Just like in so many countries throughout history, when great persecution began in Iran, that was when the church began to grow. More and more people were coming because life was terrible and they were so hungry for something true and real that offered them hope.

....

"And Israel was brought very low because of Midian. And the people of Israel cried out for help to the LORD." Judges 6:6

Dear God, help me to turn to You not just when things are terrible, but all the time. Help me to be there for other people who are looking for something true and real, so I can offer them the hope of Jesus Christ.

....

DAY 67

When he was young, George Mueller wanted to be a missionary, but God called him to be a pastor in England.

Then he began to care for the orphans around him. Through the years as he trusted God to help him care for orphans, God provided thousands and hundreds of thousands of pounds. There came a time when the orphanage had more than it needed and George could put some away in savings—but not for himself.

One day, when the news came that the Pope had finally allowed the people of Spain to read the Bible, George had saved enough money to flood the land of Spain with Bibles within a few months. He paid for booklets and missionaries too.

George Mueller was excited to be able to give to such an important work. This way, even though he didn't go to be a missionary, he could help others go.

....

"Each one must give as he has decided
in his heart, not reluctantly or under
compulsion, for God loves a cheerful
giver." 2 Corinthians 9:7

Help me to be a cheerful giver too, God,
like George Mueller. Thank You that I can
give money and time for Your work.

....

DAY 68

"Who will go be a missionary to the tribal people of your own nation?" the speaker asked the Ethiopian Christians. "Who will answer Christ's call?"

Many young men volunteered. But one of them, Fanta, was a cripple. "God has called me to the violent Oromo tribe beside Lake Abaya," he said.

"No, you can't go!" answered the missionaries. "You're a cripple! They'll kill you!"

"I must go," said Fanta. "I'm happy to give my life, but God has called me."

Who knew that the Oromo tribe honored cripples? Through Fanta's preaching, many of them came to Christ.

In Philippians Paul wrote, "I can do all things through Christ, who strengthens me." Philippians 4:13

That verse doesn't mean you'll be able to flap your arms and fly, or get away with sin. It means that, like Fanta, if God calls you to do something for Him, He'll enable you to accomplish the work He has called you to do.

....

Lord Jesus, help me to listen to Your call for me. Help me to trust You to strengthen me to do the work You've called me to do.

....

DAY 69

"What does this Scripture mean?" asked one of the Kimyal pastors. He was reading in the book of Romans.

"We were buried therefore with him by baptism into death, in order that, just as Christ was raised from the dead by the glory of the father, we too might walk in newness of life." Romans 6:4

The missionary Orin Kidd answered, "I've told you about baptism, and how it's a picture of your new life. Now, you ask the Holy Spirit to open the eyes of your understanding."

All the young men were silent, reading the Scripture and praying. Then Siud jumped up. "The Lord spoke to me! I understand it! We were in Christ when He died! We were in Christ when He rose again! Jesus has broken the power of sin in our lives! We can live holy lives in the power of the Holy Spirit!"

Siud exclaimed, "I will teach my people this Sunday!"

Did you know that when you read the Bible, you can ask the Holy Spirit to open your eyes to what the Scriptures mean? When you do, He'll help you understand things you didn't understand before.

....

Thank You, Lord, for giving us Your Holy Spirit to teach me through Your holy Scriptures. Help me to be faithful in asking for Your help when I read.

....

DAY 70

Mako never did learn to read. But he longed to take the gospel to the people of his native village in Africa, so he memorized the book of John and set out.

"I have great news!" he cried. "You no longer have to be enslaved to the spirits! The great God has sent One to free you!"

Mako repeated the entire gospel of John over and over. Some of the people listened and began to memorize it as well. One after another they fell on their faces before the true and living God, confessing their sins and claiming Jesus Christ as Savior and Lord.

You don't have to be highly educated to tell others about Jesus. The most important thing you need is a real relationship with Jesus yourself. You have to know, not just in your head but in your whole being, that He really is the Savior, that He's your Savior, and that He is the hope of the whole world.

....

Jesus said, "Blessed ... are those who hear the word of God and keep it!" Luke 11:28

Thank You, Lord God, that Your Word shows us the way of life. Help me to hear the word of God, and keep it.

....

DAY 71

Mako and his people had memorized the gospel of John, but they longed for more teaching. "Oh God, send us someone who can read and teach the Bible!" they prayed.

Months passed. The people recited the gospel of John. They sang. And they prayed. "Oh God, send us one to teach us!"

One afternoon Mako began to sob. "O faithful God!" he cried. "I've trusted You! But I've asked You for so long to send us someone to teach us more about You, and You haven't! What shall I do?" His body shook with sobbing.

Suddenly Mako saw a man standing there with a Bible. It was a missionary, come to teach them. "Oh God!" he cried. "Forgive me! I doubted Your love! But all along You had someone prepared to come. Oh thank You, God!!"

Sometimes waiting for God to do His important work can seem very long. But we can trust that He is always working.

....

Jesus prayed, "The glory that you have given me I have given to them, that they may be one even as we are one... so that the world may know that you sent me and loved them even as you loved me."
John 17:22-23

Dear Father, You delight for the world to know You and Your great love. Help me to be faithful in prayer for people like Mako who need others to come and help them.

....

DAY 72

The Karen Christians gathered for the Annual Assembly, to sing, pray, and talk together, and to call for more missionaries. "Who will go to the Brec tribe?" the leader asked. The Brecs were vicious and violent.

Su Yah said, "I will go."

"What about the wild animals on the way?" said someone.

"When I was young, God delivered me from a tiger and a bear. I'm not afraid of wild animals."

"They may kill you before you get a chance to speak," said someone.

"I know," answered Su Yah. "But what better way to die than in the service of my King?"

God is calling many to be strong and very courageous, to go to the hard places even when they look daunting. He wants us to be people of courage, trusting our lives into His hands.

Su Yah won the hearts of the Brecs . . . by singing! He preached the truth of Christ, and many believed.

....

"Be strong, and let your heart take courage, all you who wait for the LORD!"
Psalm 31:24

Father in heaven, thank You for examples of courage. Help me to be a courageous Christian too and be willing to give my life for You.

....

DAY 73

In 1979, the country of Iran underwent a massive revolution. The man who took over promised peace and plenty, but all he brought was violence and famine. The whole nation groaned under his harsh rule.

Hossein Soodmand and his wife knew the law said that anyone who converted from Islam to Christianity could be killed. But he said, "I believe God wants me to start a secret church. The people are so hungry for the truth, for peace. They need to arise and eat, just like the voice told me in the hospital." He knew that these people needed the Living Bread, Jesus Christ.

Sunday after Sunday, dozens of people came to meet in that little basement. Hundreds of them were saved.

Our country still allows people to talk about their faith in Christ. But there are many around you who are hungry for what is true. You can tell them of the Living Bread, Jesus Christ.

....

"When he saw the crowds, he had compassion for them, because they were harassed and helpless, like sheep without a shepherd." Matthew 9:36

Lord Jesus, thank You that You have compassion on the people who need a shepherd. Please provide the truth for more and more people in Iran.

....

DAY 74

"Why do you say Jesus died on purpose?" one kidnapper demanded from missionary Russell Stendal. "It would have been good enough just to give us a message about mercy and love. If I were God and came down to earth, I wouldn't let anyone nail me to a cross! I would have called down all the angels and defended myself. An all-powerful God wouldn't have let himself be put to death. This shows that you made up this story. It's a story for weaklings and fools!"

The kidnapper had no understanding at all about God's love for sinners. That's the reason Jesus died.

Russell prayed. Finally he said, "Jesus died because we've all been kidnapped." He looked at their hopeless faces. "We've been kidnapped by our own selfishness and pride. But Jesus came to die and pay the price of all our sin and rise again to break the power of sin and death. He came to set us all free."

....

"In this the love of God was made manifest among us, that God sent his only Son into the world, so that we might live through him." 1 John 4:9

Lord God, thank You so much for sending Jesus to die for us. Lord Jesus, even though You are the all-powerful God, You allowed Yourself to be put to death to set us free. Thank You.

....

DAY 75

One of the kidnappers, Mariano, hated Russell. Russell said, "You kidnapped me as an act of terrorism, but our loving and merciful God had a different reason. He loves you and wants me to tell you all about Him. Christianity isn't a system like socialism or capitalism. It's a personal relationship with God through Jesus Christ."

Christianity isn't a system. If you've grown up in a Christian home, it's important to know that this doesn't make you a Christian.

When Russell was finally able to leave, Mariano began to cry. He grabbed Russell's hand. Then he choked out, "Forgive me for the way I treated you."

It's a personal relationship with God through Christ. Mariano knew that Russell's Christianity was real. You need to have your own real relationship with God too. If you don't, don't call yourself a Christian. But if you do, you can! Call on Him today to save you and make you new, make you His.

....

"I count everything as loss because of the surpassing worth of knowing Christ Jesus my Lord." Philippians 3:8

Dear God, thank You that I can truly know You, the way Russell Stendal did, and the apostle Paul. Help me to experience more of that personal relationship.

....

DAY 76

When George Mueller wrote books, and when he traveled and spoke, he taught people how to pray.

"Once I'm sure that a thing is right and for the glory of God," he said, "I keep on praying for it until the answer comes. I don't give up!"

Have you ever prayed for something that God showed you was right and for His glory? After praying for a while, have you ever felt like giving up?

"The great fault of the children of God is that they don't keep on praying," George Mueller said. "If they would, they would see great things from God."

"Don't think that I have a special gift of faith," he preached, "Don't think that's why I'm able to trust God. I have the same faith that is in every true believer. Little by little it has been increasing over the last many years. This kind of faith can be yours."

....

"And [Jesus] told them a parable to the effect that they ought always to pray and not lose heart." Luke 18:1

Dear Lord, help me to know when a thing is right and for Your glory. Help me to keep praying and not give up. Lord, increase my faith.

....

DAY 77

Everything was going wrong for Laliso. This Ethiopian evangelist wanted to take the gospel to Goybi village. But corrupt policemen stopped him.

When he was finally released, it was night, too dangerous in the forest because of the leopards. So Laliso tried to stay on the edge of the riverbank. But in the dark, he fell in.

Does it ever seem, when you're trying to serve God, everything goes wrong? When Laliso finally found a place to climb out, he saw a village and called for help. It was Goybi village!

The villagers murmured. "A man coming to us from the water! The ancient prophecy!"

The corrupt policemen, traveling in the dark, falling into the river—all Laliso's troubles worked to fulfill a prophecy. The people were ready to hear the gospel.

When you're serving God, does it ever seem like everything is going wrong? You can trust Him. He knows what He's doing. He has a greater plan!

....

"The steps of a man are established by the LORD, when he delights in his way; though he fall, he shall not be cast headlong, for the LORD upholds his hand." Psalm 37:23-24

Thank You Lord, that when I follow You, I can trust that You know where You're leading me. Help me to continue to trust.

....

DAY 78

Javid hated the war against Iraq where he was required to fight. When other soldiers around him were killed, he escaped. He ran off to Mashhad, to pray at the Muslim shrine.

But instead, a friend took him to a completely different kind of prayer meeting. Javid listened to his friend pray. His prayer wasn't memorized and recited like Muslim prayers—this man talked as if he were actually friends with God. Other people prayed too—they all seemed to love God so much! They talked as if they really knew Him, and as if they weren't afraid that He knew all about them. Javid had never heard people pray like this.

Do you pray this way? When you pray, do you know that God loves you? Do you love Him and tell Him so? When you pray, you can talk to Him just the way you would talk to a loving Father, because that's exactly what He is.

....

Jesus said, "Behold, I stand at the door,
and knock: if any man hear my voice,
and open the door, I will come in to him,
and will sup with him, and he with me."
Revelation 3:20 KJV

Lord Jesus, thank You that You want to
have a close friendship with me. Thank You
that if I open the door to You, I can talk
with You as with a friend.

....

DAY 79

"My heart breaks for these young men, wounded in body and spirit." Pastor Hossein Soodmand was talking about the terrible war that Iran was fighting against Iraq.

Then he said to Javid, "One day you will become a bold, strong soldier in the army of God."

"What do you mean?" Javid's stomach turned at the thought of killing for God. But surely this couldn't be what Pastor Soodmand meant. Not with his kind face and gentle eyes.

Javid had no idea then that he was in a spiritual war. One day he would fight that war by becoming an evangelist. He would preach the good news of Jesus Christ, to bring others out of the kingdom of darkness.

You too are called to be a soldier in the army of God. You are called to fight against darkness and evil with the love of Jesus Christ for sinners. You have been called to an epic life.

....

"Finally, be strong in the Lord and in the strength of his might. Put on the whole armor of God, that you may be able to stand against the schemes of the devil."
Ephesians 6:10-11

Mighty God, thank You that You provide armor for Christians. Help me to put on this armor and stand against the schemes of the devil so I can bring others out of the kingdom of darkness into the kingdom of Your dear Son.

....

DAY 80

When George Mueller was seventy years old, his life calling changed. The orphans were in good care with others who worked at the orphanage. Now, instead of pastoring and caring for orphans, the Lord called him to start traveling and speaking.

Over the next seventeen years, Mr. Mueller and his wife visited forty-two countries and spoke about the life of faith to over three million people. Many people were inspired to trust God because of the life of George Mueller.

You may be looking for one specific "calling" from the Lord for your life. But your calling in your life can change. He may have one plan for you when you're young and another when you're older.

The most important thing is to never stop listening to His voice as He leads you. Keep trusting Him to show you the way, and keep seeking opportunities to make His love and care known to others.

....

"Let me hear in the morning of your steadfast love, for in you I trust. Make me know the way I should go, for to you I lift up my soul." Psalm 143:8

Thank You that I don't need to worry about the future, Lord, Thank You that I can trust You to lead me in my life. Help me to listen to Your voice for the way You want me to go.

....

DAY 81

On one of George Mueller's ocean trips from England to the U.S., the fog was so thick the captain couldn't direct the ship. "We're going to be late arriving in America," he said.

"People there are waiting to hear me speak about the faithfulness of God," said Mr. Mueller. "I must be there."

"Sorry, sir, but this fog makes it impossible," said the captain.

George Mueller took the captain down below deck and prayed, asking God to remove the fog. Finally he said, "He has done it."

When they went back up, the fog was completely gone.

How could Mr. Mueller be so sure the fog was gone? It's because he had been living a life of trusting prayer for fifty years. He had been learning what it was to trust God.

Do you want to live a life like this? Start trusting God in small ways now, and ask Him to open up bigger ways for you to trust.

....

"Trust in him at all times, O people; pour out your heart before him; God is a refuge for us." Psalm 62:8

Thank You, Father, for the example of people who have trusted You and seen You do great things. Help me to learn to trust You, for bigger and bigger works, for the glory of Your great Name.

....

DAY 82

By the time Russell Stendal was released from being held hostage, the revolutionaries had really gotten to know him, and they knew he wasn't a spy or a bad guy. The revolutionaries found out that he had used his airplane to help the farmers. He wasn't afraid of them, and he had lived as an example before them, a true example of what a Christian should be.

Some of the kidnappers actually became Russell's friends! Later he was able to visit them and talk with them more about Jesus. Some of them were saved.

You never know what kinds of opportunities the Lord will give you in your life. Live as a Christ-like example at all times. You'll mess up, just like Russell did, but if you're ready to ask God's forgiveness and change your ways, you can still be an example to others. People are longing to see an authentic faith.

"I have said these things to you, that in me you may have peace. In the world you will have tribulation. But take heart; I have overcome the world." John 16:33

Thank You, Lord, for the unexpected opportunities You give for me to be an example to others. Help me to live out an authentic faith.

DAY 83

The Bible doesn't say people will know we're Christ followers by how we keep certain rules. They'll know we're Christians by our love and kindness.

When Dick and Vida McLellan were missionaries in Ethiopia, sometimes Ethiopian boys came over and played ball with their son John. The McLellans showed kindness to the boys, gave them food and drinks, and told them about Jesus.

Many years later, Dick and two Ethiopian evangelists stood in danger of death at the hands of an angry mob. The police chief took them to the station, but they weren't sure what he would do—often the police were corrupt killers too.

But the police chief looked at Dick and said, "Are you John's father?"

Dick was surprised. "Yes."

"I was one of those boys who came to your house. You were kind to us, and you told us about Jesus. I'm glad you're teaching the Bible, and I want to help you."

....

"Beloved, let us love one another, for love is from God, and whoever loves has been born of God and knows God." 1 John 4:7

Heavenly Father, help me to show Christ by showing love to others. Help me to remember that the only way people will really know I'm Yours is by the love I have for them.

....

DAY 84

Everyone knew the Christians were the best workers at the gold mine. But they always wanted to have Sundays off for worshiping.

When the foreman said they had to start working on Sundays, all the Christians quit. But then things started going so badly at the gold mine, the foreman drove to where they were and said, "If you come back, I'll let you have Sundays off again."

But the Christians said, "Wherever we work now, we want everybody to have Sundays off, so we can teach them about God."

The foreman was irritated, but he finally agreed to let them teach the other workers about God. He knew he needed them.

Do you want to live for Christ? Then be a real Christian at all times, in your private life as well as your public life. Your character will speak about who God really is. As time passes, people will notice. God will give you more and more opportunities.

....

"One who is faithful in a very little is also faithful in much." Luke 16:10a

Dear Father, help me to be faithful in the little things so that I can be trusted with the big things too.

....

DAY 85

It was 2010. Siud, who had been just a little boy when he first thought about the Spirit who loves, was now an old man. And now, finally, the Kimyal people would receive their New Testaments in their own language. Everyone gathered for a massive celebration.

The plane landed on the airstrip the missionaries had made so many years before. The pilot took out a box and handed it to Pastor Siud.

Then Pastor Siud called for silence. "O God!" he prayed. "The plan that You had from the beginning regarding Your Kimyals has come to pass today! You decided that we should see Your Word in our own language. Today You have placed Your Word into my hands, just as You promised. I give you praise!"

The New Testament had come. The people had the Word of God in their own language. The valley erupted with cheers and singing, weeping and praising. It was a time of great celebration.

....

"I wait for the LORD, my soul waits, and in his word I hope." Psalm 130:5

Lord, thank You for Your holy Word, the Bible, in my own language. Help me never to take it for granted, but to remember that it is a precious gift from You.

....

DAY 86

Su Yah was called as a missionary to the Brec tribe, on the other side of a mountain so high that it divided two countries.

He could have stayed in the valley where it was comfortable, not only because the Brecs were fearful, but also because that mountain was extremely steep and rugged. Would you have wanted to stay in the valley?

As Su Yah climbed, though, he kept trusting in God to keep him and to lead him. When he got to the top of the mountain, he may have stayed there for a while to spend time with the Lord, admiring His creation and worshiping Him.

Being at the top of the mountain is awesome. If you're able to rest on a spiritual mountaintop, you may never want to leave. But Su Yah didn't stay there. He rejoiced in God, and then he hurried down the other side of that mountain to take the good news to others.

....

"How beautiful upon the mountains are the feet of him who brings good news, who publishes peace, who brings good news of happiness, who publishes salvation, who says to Zion, 'Your God reigns.'" Isaiah 52:7

Heavenly Father, thank You that You provide "mountaintop" experiences for Your people who follow You. Help me to not only see those, but also be willing to come down from the mountain to bring the good news to others.

....

DAY 87

Chief Ho Wi of the Brec tribe loved Su Yah's words. He asked for more Christians to come and teach his people. He ordered his men to go out and chop down the underbrush in the path all the way up the mountain. "Clear the way!" he ordered. "The true Words are coming, and I want to make a way for them."

When the missionary Alonzo Bunker came, he said, "Thank you for clearing the way for us. Now the true God says, 'Clear the way for Me! Clear the way in your hearts and in your thinking for the coming of Jesus Christ!'"

You may spend time and energy preparing for a special event. It may even be an event where the Word of the Lord will be preached. But the Lord doesn't want you just to prepare the way physically. He wants you to clear the way in your head and your heart for Him.

....

"As it is written in Isaiah the prophet, 'Behold, I send my messenger before your face, who will prepare your way, the voice of one crying in the wilderness: 'Prepare the way of the Lord, make his paths straight.'"Mark 1:2-3

O Lord, help me not to get distracted by activities that seem good. Show me how to prepare the way for You to come in my thinking and my feeling and in all my ways.

....

DAY 88

The violence in Colombia grew so great that a day came when all the missionaries had to leave. All but Russell Stendal and his family. Before long he was able to start a radio station in the empty mission station.

He knew that the war-torn nation of Colombia needed words of hope and love and truth. He knew these would be found only in Jesus Christ.

Russell had spent seven years translating the Bible into Spanish for the people of Colombia. Those years of translation work filled Russell's soul and spirit with the Word of God. Because of this, he could speak for hours on the radio without any notes. He had a deep well of truth in his spirit. The hungry, thirsty nation of Colombia eagerly listened to his voice.

What Russell accomplished can be true for anyone. You can meditate on the Word of God as he did, and develop a deep well of truth in your spirit.

....

"I will run in the way of your
commandments when you enlarge
my heart!" Psalm 119:32

Thank You, Lord, that Your Word can
enlarge my heart to love others and show
them who You are. Help me as I spend
time meditating on it, to understand it and
believe it.

....

DAY 89

Hasan never learned to read, but he listened to others read the gospel of Matthew so many times that he memorized it. He believed in Jesus Christ with all his heart.

Hasan began to travel thousands of miles around his home country of Iran with packs of gospel booklets to give away. "I'm like the sower in Matthew 13!" he said. "This is my seed! The seed is the Word of God. I'm sowing it wherever I go."

Jesus said that the Word of God is like seed sowed over earth. Some of it lands on hard, packed earth, some of it on earth where stones or thorns will hinder its growth, and some of it will land on good soil where it will grow and bear fruit. When Hasan gave away his booklets, he didn't know what kind of soil was in each person's heart. But God knows. Which kind of soil is in your heart?

....

"Now the parable is this: The seed is the
word of God." Luke 8:11

God, thank You that You care about our
hearts enough to give us Your holy Word.
Help my heart to be good soil to receive
it and bear fruit. Help me to be a sower of
Your Word.

....

DAY 90

George Mueller kept careful track of every single gift that came for the work of the orphanage, writing it all in his record books. After he died, the new orphanage director studied the books. Then he studied the books more closely. He saw that sometimes the space to tell who gave the money said this: *From a servant of the Lord Jesus who wants to lay up treasure in heaven.* These gifts had stopped coming in the spring of 1898, when Mr. Mueller had died.

When George Mueller died, all his belongings were worth only a few pounds. But he had given hundreds of thousands of pounds to the work of the Lord.

Does it seem hard sometimes, giving your money to the work of the Lord? Remember that when you spend it on non-necessities, it's going to something that won't last. When you give it to the work of the Lord, it's going to something that will last forever.

....

"And Jesus, looking at [the rich young ruler], loved him, and said to him, "You lack one thing: go, sell all that you have and give to the poor, and you will have treasure in heaven; and come, follow me."
Mark 10:21

Heavenly Father, thank You for examples of people who want to store up treasure in heaven. Help me to store up my treasure there too.

....

DAY 91

The tribal people of Papua, Indonesia, had no idea that there was a purpose for their lives. When they found out about the great salvation available through Jesus Christ, they rejoiced and burned their magic charms, their "power pieces." Now they knew their lives had a greater purpose than just surviving. Now they were free to pursue that great purpose—to glorify God and rejoice in His love.

If you've known the story of Jesus Christ your whole life, it might not seem amazing to you. But imagine never having heard it before. You would think your life is pointless, except just to have a good time, or just to survive from one day to the next.

Then you find out not only does your life have a purpose, but the God of the Universe loved you enough to send His Son to die for you. This is amazing love! This is life-changing love. This is a reason to greatly rejoice.

....

"And we have seen and testify that the Father has sent his Son to be the Savior of the world." 1 John 4:14

Thank You so much, Lord, for loving me so that You sent Your Son Jesus Christ to die and rise again for me! Help me to never forget what a wonderful gift He is.

....

DAY 92

Waja learned medicine and helped people, but in communist Ethiopia, he was thrown into prison for being a Christian. There he treated his enemies with kindness and tended their wounds.

Finally the day came when he was supposed to be released. But his name wasn't on the list.

Waja had become so well-loved in the prison that all the other prisoners began to cry out, "Free Waja! Free Waja!"

"No, brothers," he said. "I'm a prisoner of Jesus Christ. I'll stay as long as He wants me to."

But the other prisoners kept crying out, "FREE WAJA!" until he was released, even though he wasn't on the list.

There are times when it's right to get away from persecution.

Before leaving, Waja quietly gave his secret Bible to an enemy who had become his friend.

How can you treat your enemies with kindness? Is there persecution in your life that you should get away from, or do you need God's help to stand up for him?

....

"But I say to you who hear, Love your enemies, do good to those who hate you, bless those who curse you, pray for those who abuse you." Luke 6:27-28

Heavenly Father, Show me when I should get away from persecution, but please help me to love my enemies and pray for them and treat them with kindness.

....

DAY 93

Three Christian Ethiopian men stood on a hill praying for the evil Communist camp to be destroyed. They prayed and prayed and prayed. Then there came a point where all three of them believed their prayer was answered. The Communist camp was still there—they could see it. But they knew God had answered their prayer. "It is done. God has accomplished it."

The next day the camp was completely taken down. Communism was falling.

Every Christian has the same God as these three men. We can learn to pray for God's will, with confidence that He will accomplish His work. Pray until you know what God wants, and then pray for that until you're sure He has given it.

Does this seem impossible? You're on the adventure called the Christian life. As you grow as a believer, you can become more confident of God's ways and see Him do great works.

....

"And Jesus answered them, 'Have faith in God. Truly, I say to you, whoever says to this mountain, 'Be taken up and thrown into the sea,' and does not doubt in his heart, but believes that what he says will come to pass, it will be done for him. Therefore I tell you, whatever you ask in prayer, believe that you have received it, and it will be yours.'" Mark 11:22-24

Lord, help me to ask in faith for Your will to be accomplished! Thank You that I can see You do great things.

....

DAY 94

Early every morning Mananga chopped wood and hauled water for Mama Laird in Africa. Then he listened to Mama's husband preach about Jesus before doing the same again.

"Good night, Mama!" he called as the sun set. He ran off.

Weeks later, strangers appeared at the meetings. "Where did you hear about our meetings?" Mr. Laird asked.

"From Mananga," they replied.

Mama asked, "Mananga, when have you been going to these other villages?"

"At night, after sunset."

"But the leopards come out at night! And weren't you exhausted from your work?"

"Mama," said Mananga, "you came here with the gospel of Christ, even though it was dangerous, and you get tired too. I have to do the same. The good news must go out."

Mananga had his priorities straight! Even when we're tired, even when it seems dangerous, we show love to others by telling them about the hope they can have in Jesus.

....

"For what we proclaim is not ourselves, but Jesus Christ as Lord, with ourselves as your servants for Jesus' sake." 2 Corinthians 4:5

Heavenly Father, by the power of Your Holy Spirit help me to have this kind of love, and to pour it out to others.

....

DAY 95

When Mananga grew up, he was as fearless as when he was young. When he preached the gospel, it made some people angry. Wicked men beat him up and nearly killed him.

At the hospital, Mananga was told he would never walk again. When his attackers were found, Mananga gave them the gospel again and freely forgave them both.

The hospital administrator listened to all this with surprise. He went to the place where Mananga had been beaten and heard how the villagers loved and respected him. They had even stopped fighting because of Mananga! The administrator bought a New Testament, read it all, and later came to Christ.

The Bible talks about the Christian life being like a race of following Christ, to keep believing, keep trusting, keep living the Christ life. This isn't a life lived by good works. It's a life lived by faith in Jesus Christ. Mananga lived that life.

....

"Let us run with endurance the race that is set before us, looking to Jesus, the founder and perfecter of our faith, who for the joy that was set before him endured the cross, despising the shame, and is seated at the right hand of the throne of God."
Hebrews 12:1b-2

Dear God, thank You for the life of faith that others before me have lived as my examples. Help me to be faithful to follow in that very same life of faith.

....

DAY 96

After Mananga was beaten, he became so sick the doctors said he would die. In that part of Africa, no one would visit the home where a dying person lay. It was a House of Death.

"Father, make this house different," he prayed. "Bring me people so I can tell them about Jesus even when I'm dying."

Later people came to Mama Laird for Bible training and she asked them, "Where did you hear about Jesus?"

"In Mananga's house of death," they replied. "I came to Jesus Christ there." Almost three hundred of them!

There came a time when people stopped coming to Mananga's house. "Lord," he prayed, "if they won't come to me, I have to go to them, to tell them about You. Will You heal me?"

And God did heal him! Mananga went on for many years to tell many people in the Central African Republic about the mighty works of God through our Savior, Jesus Christ.

....

"As it is written, 'Therefore I will praise you among the Gentiles, and sing to your name.' And again it is said, 'Rejoice, O Gentiles, with his people.' And again, 'Praise the Lord, all you Gentiles, and let all the peoples extol him.'" Romans 15:9b-11

God, help me to have a passion for souls the way Mananga did. Do mighty works for Your glory through me too!

....

DAY 97

In Colombia, the revolutionaries wanted to show their power by killing and destroying. Almost everyone lived in great fear of them.

But some of them went to prison. There they heard a man named Alex tell his testimony. Some revolutionaries had killed everyone on his bus, and they thought Alex was dead too. But he just barely survived. Now he was visiting the prison to tell how Jesus had saved him and given him the power to forgive.

There was a gasp from the prisoners. One of the revolutionaries who had killed those people on that bus was right there in that prison!

Would you have been able to say those words, "I forgive you?"

"I forgive you," said Alex.

The revolutionaries realized that the real power wasn't in the killing. It was in the ability to love and forgive those who had killed. God saved many revolutionaries that day.

....

"Be kind to one another, tenderhearted, forgiving one another, as God in Christ forgave you." Ephesians 4:32

O Lord, I know that in my life I might have to forgive some really big things. I pray that You'll give me the power to forgive as I think about my own forgiveness in Christ.

....

DAY 98

Tribal Chief Ho Wi was a Christian now. Then he found out that another village who hated God was planning to attack them.

"What will we do?" he asked. "If we fight with weapons of war, we're saying we believe Yuwah can't defend us."

"And if we kill them," Su Yah added, "they'll die in their sins without a chance to believe on Jesus Christ."

What if you knew you were going to be attacked by enemies of God? Would you be willing to consider their eternal souls?

Su Yah stopped to think. "Here's how we'll fight. I'll write letters to the pastors and elders, asking everyone to pray and keep praying. A battle of the spirits must be fought with weapons of the Spirit."

Every day the villagers prayed together. "O Yuwah, show Yourself strong to the other villages of the Brecs!" They didn't want to fight in the power of the flesh, but of the Spirit.

....

"For though we walk in the flesh, we are not waging war according to the flesh. For the weapons of our warfare are not of the flesh but have divine power to destroy strongholds." 2 Corinthians 10:3-4

Thank You, Lord, that You are far more powerful than weapons of war. Help me to remember that my first reaction to persecution should be prayer.

....

DAY 99

The enemy village kidnapped two boys from Chief Ho Wi's village. Hundreds of Christians prayed together. Then two men went and said, "In the name of the living God, return the boys you stole!" The chief refused. But all his villagers were afraid of the living God.

The Christians left, but came back the next day and said the same thing. When the chief refused, they left without a word. The chief's wife feared they would all die. The chief feared too.

The Christians prayed together again. This time, when some men walked to the enemy village, they sang, prayed, and preached. Finally the chief returned the boys.

Soon a message came to the Christians from many villages. "Send us teachers. We want to become followers of Jesus Christ."

When the Holy Spirit wins the battle, the people of the enemy become the people of God. This is how we can be "more than conquerors."

....

"No, in all these things we are more than
conquerors through him who loved us."
Romans 8:37

Thank You, Father, that love is stronger than
hate. Show me in my own life how I can
be more than a conqueror through Jesus
Christ my Lord.

....

DAY 100

The Christians in the small Iranian church were frightened. There, coming in the door, was Taher, a man who had abused and threatened to kill his Christian wife and children, a man who had hated all of them.

These Christians had helped Taher's family to escape from him. And they had been praying for him.

"Why have you come?" one asked.

"I had a dream," said Taher. "Three times I had it. A man came on a donkey and said he would cleanse me of my sins. Then another man in my dream told me it was Jesus. I have to understand."

The Christians were shocked—and excited. God had answered their prayers!

Do you ever feel like God isn't hearing, isn't answering your prayers? Keep trusting, asking, seeking and knocking.

Taher was saved and was later reunited with his family. Together they work to give others the gospel of Jesus Christ.

....

"And I tell you, ask, and it will be given to you; seek, and you will find; knock, and it will be opened to you. For everyone who asks receives, and the one who seeks finds, and to the one who knocks it will be opened." Luke 11:9-10

Thank You, Father, for Your answers to prayer. Help me not to give up praying for others, but to keep asking, seeking, and knocking.

....

DAY 101

You may never have heard of many of the missionaries and evangelists in this book. Most of them aren't well known. None of them are rich. But that doesn't mean that they're not a success.

True success isn't success in this temporary world, but success in the eternal world. That means that God doesn't care about the success of having lots of Facebook friends or Instagram followers. He doesn't care at all about the success of looking cool or being popular or having lots of money and expensive possessions.

What God cares about is success in the things that are eternal. The things that will last forever, like people's souls. He cares about faithfulness, truth, kindness, goodness, and Christlikeness.

In those ways, each of the people in this book was a great success. They focused on the things that were eternally important.

When they enter heaven, God will say, "Well done, good and faithful servant."

....

"Well done, good and faithful servant. You have been faithful over a little; I will set you over much. Enter into the joy of your master." Matthew 25:23

Lord, show me how to focus on the things that are of eternal value. May my life be a success not by the world's standards, but in Your eyes. Amen.

....

FURTHER READING

The stories in *101 Devotions for Guys* are inspired by other books written by Rebecca Davis.

With Two Hands: Stories of God at Work in Ethiopia (Hidden Heroes #1) .

The Good News Must Go Out: Stories of God at Work in the Central African Republic (Hidden Heroes #2)

Witness Men: True Stories of God at Work in Papua, Indonesia (Hidden Heroes #3).

Return of the White Book: True Stories of God at Work in Southeast Asia (Hidden Heroes #4).

Lights in a Dark Place: True Stories of God at Work in Colombia (Hidden Heroes #5).

Living Water in the Desert: True Stories of God at Work in Iran (Hidden Heroes #6).

Joy Ridderhof: Voice Catcher Around the World (Potter's Wheel Books #2).

George Mueller: Pickpocket to Praying Provider (Potter's Wheel Books #3).

Brother Yun: The Heavenly Man of China (Potter's Wheel Books #4).

Hidden Heroes Series
by Rebecca Davis

With Two Hands
Stories of God at Work in Ethiopia
ISBN: 978-1-84550-539-4

The Good News Must Go Out
True Stories of God at Work in the Central
African Republic
ISBN: 978-1-84550-628-5

Witness Men
True Stories of God at Work in Papua, Indonesia
ISBN: 978-1-78191-515-8

Return of the White Book
True Stories of God at Work in Southeast Asia
ISBN: 978-1-78191-292-8

Lights in a Dark Place
True Stories of God at Work in Columbia
ISBN: 978-1-78191-409-0

Living Water in the Desert
True Stories of God at Work in Iran
ISBN: 978-1-78191-563-9

CHRISTIAN FOCUS PUBLICATIONS

Christian Christian CF4K Mentor
Focus Heritage

Christian Focus Publications publishes books for adults and children under its four main imprints: Christian Focus, CF4K, Mentor and Christian Heritage. Our books reflect our conviction that God's Word is reliable and Jesus is the way to know him, and live for ever with him.

Our children's publication list includes a Sunday School curriculum that covers pre-school to early teens, and puzzle and activity books. We also publish personal and family devotional titles, biographies and inspirational stories that children will love.

If you are looking for quality Bible teaching for children then we have an excellent range of Bible stories and age-specific theological books.

From pre-school board books to teenage apologetics, we have it covered!

Find us at our web page:
www.christianfocus.com

CF4•K
*Because you're never
too young to know Jesus*